IDENTITY
RESTORED

delsographics

Published by Delso Graphics
E-mail: info@delsographics.com
www.delsographics.com
+27 813 925 418

Paperback ISBN: 978-0-620-87879-1
Kindle eBook ISBN: 978-0-620-88095-4

SOCIAL MEDIA INFORMATION
Instagram: mike_ayeni | Facebook: Michael Ayeni
Linkedin: Michael Ayeni | Twitter: @mikeayeni
www.pstmiketl.com | info@pstmiketl.com

TRANSFORMING LIVES
With Pst Mike

Printed in South Africa

Dedication.

Dear reader,

God had you in mind when this book was written. He longed for you to discover your identity in Him and live a life full of purpose here on earth and into eternity.

Therefore, it is not a coincidence that you have this book in your hands. To you, I dedicate this book!

Acknowledgment

I am grateful to God for the wonderful people He has placed in my life.

My praying mother, Pastor (Mrs.) Stella Ayeni. Thank you for hearing God's purpose for my life and for directing my steps according to His purpose.

My pastors, Rev Niyi and Pastor Deola Eboda; you have shaped my life and helped me learn these truths.

My lovely wife, Baxolile Thelma Ayeni; thank you for your help, partnership and support to the vision and assignment.
My great and beloved sons, Joseph and Daniel; you added beauty to my world.

Esme Witbooi, my dear daughter in the Lord and protégée; your commitment to advancing these teachings has changed the lives of many.

Rick Warren, in whose book, "The Purpose Driven Life", I discovered the reason for my existence.

My editor, Martin van Aswegen; your editing skills made this book a delight to read.

My designer, Hakeem Babatunde; your professionalism gave this book the touch of excellence.

To all my family and friends; I thank God for the privilege of sharing this book with you.

Content

Introduction

The human species is considered to be the most intelligent of all species on the planet earth. As a matter of fact, biology puts man on the top of the food chain. But man, since creation has proven himself to be the most confused of all species. Why is this? Scientists have made and are still making great discoveries in the animal and plant world. They have made giant strides in identifying the nature and uniqueness of various plants and animals but humanity is still on the endless search for its own identity. It could take an individual a lifetime to discover his or her own identity and purpose for existence.

The search for man's identity is as old as mankind. Man, through evolution, psychology and philosophy, has propounded and postulated theories and ideologies to explain his identity but these have only led to an endless, futile and dead-end search for his true identity. Only God's Word holds the key to unlocking, discovering, unravelling and restoring man's true identity. The purpose of this book is to help you discover your identity.

The world's population was estimated to have reached 7.8 billion as of December 2019. According to science, each person has their own unique and distinct fingerprints. Therefore, we have over 7.8 billion different fingerprints on earth. Even identical twins don't have the same fingerprints.

It means God created everyone to be different, distinct and unique.

Trying to be like someone else will only make you end up as a photocopy or a counterfeit.

Trying to exist like someone else will only make you the second best and put you in second place in life. You have a race to run in life called purpose. It is not a race to compete, but to complete. Only you can win your race in life.

One of life's greatest compete tragedies is to end your race only to realize that you ran in another's man track. Stay in your place. Only you can be you. There is authenticity and uniqueness in your identity.

Let's go and discover your identity!

1

DEFINING YOUR IDENTITY
WHO AM I?

Before we embark on this explorative journey of discovering your identity, let us start with defining the word "identity".

Identity is the characteristic of determining who or what a person or thing is. This definition fits the purpose and context of this book.

Through the course of this book, we will be looking at the different attributes, elements, characteristics and nature that make a person who and what they are.

2

WHERE DID
I
COME FROM?

The journey of discovering your true identity starts with discovering the source of your identity, i.e. where you really come from. When asked where you come from, you might point to your family, race, nationality or ethnicity as your origin. While this may be a biological fact, where you originally come from transcends family, race, nationality or ethnicity. So where do you really come from?

> *Then God said, "Let Us make man in Our image, according to Our likeness... So God created man in His own image; in the image of God He created him; male and female He created them. Genesis 1:26-27 (NKJV)*

The Scripture above is telling us that God is the source of man's identity - God is where you originally come from.

GOD CREATED ME

The following scriptural thoughts will shed more light on the importance of understanding and acknowledging God as the source of your identity.

- When God created plants, He spoke to the earth and plants came out of the earth (Genesis 1:11-12).
- When God created fish, He spoke to the water and the water teemed with fish (Genesis 1:20).
- But When God created man, He did not speak to the earth or water, He spoke to Himself and man came out of God (Genesis 1:26-27).

Plants came from the earth. Fish came from water. Man came from God.

For a plant to stay alive, it must remain in the earth where it came from. Outside earth, the plant dies.

For the fish to stay alive, it must remain in the water where it came from. Outside water, the fish dies.

For man to stay alive, he must remain in God where he came from. Outside God, man dies. Why?

The source of anything is the sustainer of that thing.

The following Scriptures stress the importance of knowing and having Christ who is the source of life.

> *He who has the Son has life; he who does not have the Son of God does not have life. 1 John 5:12 (NKJV).*

> *For in Him we live and move and have our being, as also some of your own poets have said, 'For we are also His Offspring -Acts 17:28 (NKJV).*

> *The thief does not come except to steal, and to kill, and to destroy. I have come that they may have life, and that they may have it more abundantly John 10:10 (NKJV).*

From the Scriptures above, we can deduce that;

- In Christ, Man is alive.
- Outside Christ, man is dead.
- If we live in Him, then we are dead outside Him.

The abundant life according to John 10:10, does not refer to the quantity of the life that you live but to its quality. A quality life is a life of purpose, meaning, significance and relevance. And this kind of life can only be found and lived in Christ who is the source of life.

Outside Christ, life is dead. Death in this context does not mean the cessation of life but a life that lacks purpose, meaning, significance and relevance.

Living a life of purpose, meaning, significance and relevance starts with you discovering your identity in Christ.

The day you were born was the day you began to exist. But the day you discover your identity (who you are) is the day you begin to live.

Man has not lived until he discovers himself, and man cannot discover himself outside God.

ESTABLISHING YOUR IDENTITY WHAT AM I?

Now that you have been able to discover God as the source of your identity, let us take our journey further, this time to discover the attributes of your identity.

Let's start by discovering the substance of your identity; in other words, what your identity is made of. To discover what your identity is made of, you need to understand the nature of God in you.

I AM A BEING CREATED IN THE IMAGE OF GOD

> *So God created man in His own image; in the image of God He created him; male and female He created them. Genesis 1:27 (NKJV).*

Biology affirms that children carry the genotype and phenotype of their parents. It further stresses that the "DNA" of a parent will always be found in his or her child. According to Genesis 1:27, you are a product of God's image and likeness, therefore, you carry God's nature in your identity.

I AM SPIRIT

John 4:24 says *"God is Spirit, and those who worship Him must worship in spirit and truth."* God who is Spirit made you in His Spirit-image and likeness. Therefore, the substance of your identity is spirit. This makes you a Spirit being.

Like children carry the genes of their parents, 1 Corinthians 3:16 says the Spirit of God dwells in you. God is not human, He is Spirit. Therefore, your spiritual nature gives you the capacity to relate to and fellowship with God's Spirit. This is what Jesus meant when He said in John 4:24, *"...those who worship Him must worship in spirit and truth."*

Worshiping God in spirit does not necessarily mean speaking in tongues; it means worshiping God in your true nature - in spirit. God is neither white nor black. He is Spirit. The color of your skin (white or black), does not make you closer to God. *Acts 10:34, "Then Peter opened his mouth, and said, 'Of a truth I perceive that God is no respecter of persons'" (KJV).* Your nationality, race or status (rich or poor), does not make you closer to God. Romans 10:12 says, *"For there is no difference between the Jew and the Greek: for the same Lord over all is rich unto all that call upon him."* God is Spirit. What makes you closer to God is your spirit - God's nature in you.

This analogy will further buttress the thought that you take after God's spiritual nature –

Animals reproduce after their kind, plants reproduce after their kind, humans reproduce after their kind. A lion gives birth to a lion. An apple seed, when planted will produce an apple tree. Humans give birth to humans. As you know by now that God is not human but spirit. Romans 8:16 says, *"The Spirit Himself bears witness with our spirit that we are children of God."* God is a parent, He has children. God who is Spirit will certainly reproduce after His kind.

Job 33:4 says *"the Spirit of God has made me, and the breath of the Almighty gives me life."* Therefore, if a lion gives birth to a lion, an apple seed when planted produces an apple tree, and humans give birth to humans, God who is Spirit will certainly give birth to a spirit-man. Jesus affirmed this by saying; in John 3:6, *"that which is born of the flesh is flesh, and that which is born of the Spirit is spirit."* God is a Spirit being and therefore you are a spirit being. You are first and foremost a spirit being before you are a human being.

I have a Spirit Nature.
It is not enough to know God created you a spirit being; you need to understand what it means to be a spirit being. If you were asked in an interview or in any social setting, to introduce and describe your personality, would you just introduce yourself based on your gender – "I am a man" or "I am a woman"? Would this information be enough to describe who you are? Certainly not! Therefore, calling yourself a spirit being is not enough to describe your spirit nature. You need to understand the attributes of your spirit nature.

To understand your spirit nature, you need to know the attributes of God's spirit because you were made from His Spirit. What exactly are the attributes of God's Spirit?" This Scripture will show you:

> *The Spirit of the Lord shall rest upon Him, The Spirit of wisdom and understanding, The Spirit of counsel and might, The Spirit of knowledge and of the fear of the Lord (Isaiah 11:2) NKJV.*

The attributes of God's Spirit as reflected in Isaiah 11:2 are referred to as the seven-fold attributes of the Spirit of God by Bible theologians;

The Spirit of the Lord	The Spirit of wisdom
The Spirit of understanding	The Spirit of counsel
The Spirit of might	The Spirit of knowledge and

The Spirit of the fear of the Lord.

Your spirit was made from the Spirit of the Lord and therefore possesses these attributes. When God was creating you in His Spirit image and likeness, He was busy depositing these attributes of His Spirit in your spirit. The Spirit of the Lord Himself and all His attributes which include wisdom, understanding, counsel, might, knowledge and fear (also known as reverence) are in you. It is here, then, that you will see the uniqueness of your spirit nature.

You were created to be wise, not foolish. Therefore, your spirit should reflect the wisdom of God in your field of expertise. From the wealth of God's wisdom residing in your spirit, you should be able to innovate cutting-edge ideas, strategies and inventions that will transform your sphere of influence. You should be able to proffer solutions to the problems confronting our world. You have God's wisdom for creativity resident in you. Ephesians 3:10 **says *"to the intent that now the manifold wisdom of God might be made known by the church to the principalities and powers in the heavenly places."*** The universe is waiting for you to display God's wisdom in you.

Your spirit should reflect understanding, not confusion. Why? 1 Corinthians 14:33 says, *"For God is not the author of confusion but of peace..."* What God has not authored should not be an authority in your life. You have the Spirit of understanding in you to understand difficult problems and solve them. You don't need to be confused when problems arise, God has given you the ability to solve them. Your spirit should reflect knowledge, not ignorance. This knowledge comes through studying God's Word. 2 Timothy 2:15 says *"Study to show thyself approved unto God, a workman that needed not to be ashamed, rightly dividing the word of truth."* You should have a sound knowledge of who God is, who you are and His purpose for creating you. You should also abound in knowledge in your field of expertise.

Your spirit should reflect counsel. Another word for counsel is advice. You should be able to give and receive godly advice. Proverbs 20:18 says, *"Plans are established by counsel; by wise counsel wage war."* Proverbs 15:22 says *"Plans fail for lack of counsel, but with many advisers they succeed."* A man is not wise if he is too wise to be counseled.

Your spirit should reflect might (also known as strength). Ephesians 3:16 says *"that He would grant you, according to the riches of His glory, to be strengthened with might through His Spirit in the inner man."* The inner man refers to your spirit. You should be able to draw strength from the reservoir of God's Spirit of might dwelling in your spirit to run your daily affairs and pursue your dreams and goals. Ephesians 6:10 says, *"Finally, my brethren, be strong in the Lord and in the power of His might."*

Your spirit should reflect the fear of God in all you do. This is not a scary kind of fear. This fear means to reverence and acknowledge God in all you do. Proverbs 3:6 says, *"in all your ways acknowledge Him, and He shall direct your paths."*

To reverence God is to have a great respect for God. To reverence God is to reflect His character in all you do. A life that reverences God is a life that says, "If God is not there, I don't want to be there. If God is not involved in it, I don't want to be involved in it. If doing it will break God's heart, then I will not do it because I have too much respect for God."

I have a God-Nature.
Your God-nature is another key attribute of your identity. To affirm that you have a God-nature, let's use the same analogy we used to affirm your spiritual nature. If animals, plants and humans produce after their kind, what kind do you think God will produce?

Let's take it further. Romans 8:16 says, *"The Spirit Himself bears witness with our spirit that we are children of God."* So God is a parent and He has children.

Now, if lions give birth to lions, an apple seed, when planted produces an apple tree and humans give birth to humans, who or what do you think God will give birth to? Think about this for a moment.

Done thinking? What did you come up with? Let's see if your thoughts agree with mine.

Now, if lions give birth to lions, an apple seed, when planted produces apple fruits and humans give birth to humans, God will certainly give birth to gods. Now before you shut the book and scream blasphemy, read the Scripture that supports this truth.
Psalm 82:6 says, *"I said, "You are gods, and all of you are children of the Most High."*
Jesus re-emphasized this Scripture thousands of years later. In John 10:34-35, He said, when answering the Jews, *"Is it not written in your law, 'I said, 'You are gods?" If he called them gods, to whom the word of God came and the Scripture cannot be broken..."*

2 Corinthians 13:1 says, *"In the mouth of two or three witnesses shall every word be established."* It was mentioned twice in the Bible that you are a god, so it is established that you have a God-nature. No one, including the devil, and not even you, can change your God-nature.

But why would God call you a god? Because you are His child. He gave birth to you from Himself. Being a child of God is a relational and revelational affair, not a religious affair. This is a scriptural revelation of your godly identity.

When Jesus said this, the religious leaders and people wanted to stone him to death because their religious mindset could not comprehend this revelation. I hope you do not want to do the same?

By calling you a god, the Bible (Jesus Himself), does not imply that you are a deity or an idol that needs to be worshipped –absolutely not! Doing that would be idolatry. All Jesus was saying is that you have a godly nature because God gave birth to you. 2 Peter 1:4 says *"...you may be partakers of the divine nature."* Which divine nature is this? 1 Corinthians 3:16 says your body is God's temple. God living in you makes your nature divine and godly. There is divinity in your humanity.

God as God will certainly reproduce after His kind. Therefore, the substance of your identity is not only spirit, it is also godly. Regardless of how much we try to fight this truth, deny it, or argue it, Jesus said, the Scripture cannot be broken; you are a god-being! Accept it - it's who you are.

The devil has kept a lot of believers bound for decades because of their ignorance of this truth. But in John 8:32, 36; Jesus said, *"...you will know the truth and the truth will make you free."* And, *"if the Son makes you free, you will be free indeed."* Your knowledge of your spiritual and godly identity will liberate you from your identity crisis, low self-esteem or any of the lies that the devil tells you, saying that you are no good.

Before you read the next session, please say this confession.

> "I am created in the image of God and after His likeness.
> And God is Spirit, therefore, I am spirit.
> I have the attributes of His Spirit in me.
> I have the Spirit of the Lord in me.
> I have the Spirit of wisdom in me.
> I have the Spirit of understanding in me.
> I have the Spirit of counsel in me.
> I have the Spirit of might in me.
> I have the Spirit of knowledge in me and
> I have the Spirit of the fear of the Lord in me.
> God created me after His image and likeness,
> therefore, I am godly.
> I have His divine nature in me.
> I am no longer bound to identity crises, low self-esteem or any lies of the devil telling me that I am no good.
> I am wonderfully and fearfully made.
> I am a child of God.
> I am free!"

I AM HUMAN

Now that we have been able to discover your spirit and godly nature, the question we must ask is, "Where is your human nature in this picture?" Your human nature and the role it plays in your whole identity makeup is what we will be looking at in this section.

Let us start with considering two Scriptures:

> *Then God said, "Let Us make man in Our image, according to Our likeness... So God created man in His own image... "Genesis 1:26-27 (NKJV)*

> *And the Lord God formed man of the dust of the ground, and breathed into his nostrils the breath of life; and man became a living being. Genesis 2:7 (NKJV)*

The first Scripture says that God created man and second Scripture says that God formed man. After reading both Scriptures, you might want to ask; "God, how many "men" did you create?" Don't be confused, God did not create two different "men". The man of Genesis 1:26-27 is the spirit-man while the man of Genesis 2:7 is the body-man. In 2 Corinthians 4:16, Paul calls it the "outward man" and the "inner man".

Note that the body-man was formed from the dust of the ground, not from God's Spirit. After God formed the body-man, it was lifeless. It wasn't until God breathed into his nostrils the breath of life that he became alive. The question is, "What did God breathe into the body-man that gave it life?" James 2:26 says, *"the body without the spirit is dead.* "This means it is the spirit that gives life to the body.

So what God breathed into the body-man was the spirit-man. The body-man is a container for the spirit man. Just as your clothes cover your body, so your body covers your spirit. When a man dies, they say he is gone but his body is lying there at the funeral. Who is gone? It is his spirit - the real him - that is gone. So, you are not just your body.

Why did God give you a body? God had a purpose for you to fulfill on the earth, so He had to make a container for you, and that container is your body. Your body gives you the ability to function on the earth. It was written concerning Jesus in Hebrews 10:5&7, *"Therefore, when He came into the world, He said... a body You have prepared for Me.... To do Your will, O God."* You can see that there is a "body" and there is a "Me". The "Me" is Jesus and the "body" is His container. When God sent Jesus to the earth, He had to give him a body to do His will on the earth. So God gave us a body to do His will on the earth.

There is so much hype in today's world to have a perfect and healthy body. People are more concerned about their body than their spirit. It is amazing how so many people attach so much value to making their body look right, but neglect their spirit. However, the value of a product is not in the container, but in the content. No matter how beautiful a bottle of coke looks; without the content, it is useless. Your spirit is the content that gives your body value. And until you discover your spirit-nature, whatever you do or wear to make your body look right is still useless. Some people will go to any length - even entering into debt - to buy good clothes so as to fit in or project an identity. Good clothes don't give you identity, they only make you broke. Your spirit is the place where your true identity lies.

So many people think fame and fortune will give them identity, but they cannot. You can have fame and fortune and still be confused about who you are. Jesus said *"for one's life does not consist in the abundance of the things he possesses" (Luke 12:15).* Your value is not in your valuables. You can make a huge amount of money and still have no meaning. Who you are is not what you see on the outside, it is who you are on the inside. Face value can be fake value. The process of discovering and restoring your identity starts internally not externally.

An identity crisis or low self-esteem is a human nature that has been conditioned by very harsh circumstances. When a particular race of people has been marginalized and subjected to oppression or victimization over a long period of time by another race, they might begin to see themselves as inferior to their oppressors. Why? They have been mentally conditioned to see themselves as inferior. But this is another lie of the devil. God created man (not a particular race) in his own image. Romans 10:12 says *"For there is no distinction between Jew and Greek, for the same Lord over all is rich to all who call upon Him."* Galatians 3:28 says, *"There is neither Jew nor Greek, there is neither slave nor free, there is neither male nor female; for you are all one in Christ Jesus."* The color of your skin does not make you closer or farther from God.

God is a Spirit not a color. You relate with God with your spirit not with the color of your skin. If you take balloons of different colors, put air inside them and release them, they will all fly. What makes a balloon fly is not the color of the balloon, but the air inside the balloon. Success in life has nothing to do with the color of your skin, it has everything to do with the discovery of your God-given identity in Christ.

An identity crisis, from a biological point of view, has to do with the situation surrounding your birth or the environment you grew up in. Children who grew up in psychologically-debilitating environments and in broken homes where they experienced abuse, lack of parental affirmation, love, care and support will struggle with identity crisis and low self-esteem in their teenage and adult life. But Rick Warren said in his book, The Purpose Driven Life, "while there are illegitimate parents, there are no illegitimate children. Many children might not be planned by their parents, but they are not unplanned by God."

You might not have a father, but you have God the Father. David said, *"You formed my inward parts and covered me in my mother's womb." (Psalm 139:13)*. God said to Jeremiah that He knew him before he was formed in his mother's womb and He had a purpose for his life before he was born (Jeremiah 1:4-5). Your identity and purpose predated your conception in your mother's womb. God used your mother's womb to cover you with flesh not to give you an identity or purpose. Myles Munroe said, "You are purpose covered with flesh." You must look past your mother's womb and take your identity from God.

You must redefine how you see yourself and what you call yourself. See yourself how God sees you and call yourself what God calls you. David said, *"I will praise You, for I am fearfully and wonderfully made." (Psalm 139:14)*. You are fearfully and wonderfully made. The events surrounding your birth might seem to be a mistake but you are not a mistake. Why? Because God never creates mistakes, He only creates miracles! You are a miracle!

I AM BLESSED
Let's look at two Scriptures that tell us about the blessing of God.

> *God has blessed us with every spiritual blessing in the heavenly places in Christ. (Ephesians 1:3).*

In this Scripture, we see that God's blessing is of a spiritual nature.

> *So God created man in His own image; in the image of God He created him; male and female He created them. Then God blessed them, and God said to them, "Be fruitful and multiply; fill the earth and subdue it..." Genesis 1:27-28 (NKJV).*

I would like you to note the underlined words in this Scripture. Who were the "them" that God blessed? The "them" here speaks about the spirit-man. After God created the spirit-man, he blessed him. So the spirit-man is blessed. You are actually a blessing-covered flesh. The blessing of God is in your spirit, not on your body. So stop attaching your blessing to what you have or don't have. Stop attaching your blessing to what you wear, drive, where you live or the kind of job you have. If you do that, you are belittling the blessing of God. God's blessing is beyond material ephemeral things.

Deuteronomy 28:3 says *"Blessed shall you be in the city, and blessed shall you be in the country."* God did not say you shall be blessed because of the city and because of the country; He said, blessed shall you be in the city and in the country. It means, the city and the country are blessed because of you. Your house is blessed because of you. Your clothes are blessed because of you. Your car is blessed because of you. Your job or the company you work for is blessed because of you. How? You are the Blessed! So stop defining, qualifying or quantifying yourself by these ephemeral things - you are the Blessed. Jesus said, *"for one's life does not consist in the abundance of the things he possesses" Luke 12:15.* Your value is not in your valuables. Therefore, don't go into debt to buy clothes, shoes and jewellery just to be beautiful. These things don't make you beautiful, they make you broke. Stop trying to impress people who are not even watching you. You are the Blessed!

What is the blessing? The blessing is an empowerment to succeed in all that you do. God's blessing is spiritual and it is resident in your spirit-man. Therefore, your spirit-man has been empowered to succeed before you appeared on this earth. So we can boldly declare that God wanted to bless the earth and He sent you as a blessing to the earth.

You are not cursed - no! Christ redeemed you from the curse over two thousand years ago (Galatians 3:13-14). You are a blessing. And no one can curse you because you were created by God to be a blessing. Numbers 23:8 brings it home; **"How shall I curse whom God has not cursed?"**

Therefore, having this knowledge that the blessing of God is in your spirit-man, do you realize that you don't acquire the blessing on the earth, you produce it? Put a blessed man in the desert, he will produce the blessing there. The desert will be blessed because of him. Psalm 118:26 says *"Blessed is he who comes in the name of the Lord! We have blessed you from the house of the Lord."* You came in the name of the Lord as a blessing to this earth. You were blessed from God's house to be a blessing on this earth. The earth is blessed because of you.

When you fully comprehend and internalize this truth that you are the blessed, no force in hell can keep you down. Regardless of how impoverished the community or nation you live in is, or the family you were born into, you can still produce the blessing. When you plant a mango seed on a garbage heap, the mango seed will produce mango not garbage. A seed produces after its nature not after its environment. You carry the nature of God's blessing in you to produce the BLESSING!

I HAVE AUTHORITY

Jesus said, *"But if I cast out demons by the Spirit of God, surely the kingdom of God has come upon you"* *Matthew 12:28.* The Spirit of God has the authority to cast out devils. Job said, *"The Spirit of God has made me..."* *Job 33:4.* Isn't it mind-blowing to know that you are a product of the Spirit of God who has the authority to cast out demons?

1 Corinthians 3:16 says, *"Do you not know that you are the temple of God and that the Spirit of God dwells in you?"* And where God's Spirit dwells, no demon is permitted to dwell there. God's Spirit dwells in you, therefore no demon or devil is permitted to dwell in you. Do not permit any demon or demonic problems to interfere with you. Whenever you sense any demonic attack or interference with your body, cast it out, saying, "Only God's Spirit is permitted to dwell in my body, so get OUT and get LOST in Jesus' name!"

1 John 4:4 says, *"You are of God, little children, and have overcome them, because He who is in you is greater than he who is in the world."* Who is the "He" in you that is greater than the "he" in the world? Colossians 1:27 says... *"Christ in you..."* So Christ is in you and is greater than any devil in the world. Philippians 2:9-11 says every knee bows to Jesus and He to whom every knee bows, lives in you! Luke 4:18 and Acts 10:38 talk about Jesus setting the oppressed free. And this same Jesus lives in you. If Jesus lives in you, you should be the setting the oppressed free - you should not be the oppressed.

There is an animal in the jungle that symbolizes authority anywhere. It is the lion. Other animals dread this majestic animal. When it walks, it walks with authority. In Revelation 5:5, Jesus is called the Lion of the tribe of Judah. This title is used to symbolize Jesus's authority - an authority that other demons dread. Proverbs 28:1 says, *"...the righteous are bold as a lion."*

You are the righteousness of God according to 2 Corinthians 5:21, so you have the same lion-like anointing that Jesus has because you belong to His tribe. When a lion sleeps, it sleeps with confidence. Animals are wary of even a sleeping lion. You would not dare to walk by a sleeping lion.

A lion looks dangerous and commands the same authority whether it is awake or asleep. If the Bible says the righteous are bold as a lion, it means demons should be scared of you whether you are awake or sleeping. It is an insult on your redemptive authority to be oppressed by the devil in your sleep. Cast him out!

It is time for you to stop running away from the devil. Proverbs 30:30 says, *"A lion, which is mighty among beasts and does not turn away from any."* You have been running from a devil that should be running from you. Turn back now and cast him out of your life, marriage, children family and home. James 2:19 says, *"You believe that there is one God. You do well. Even the demons believe and tremble!"*

UNDERSTANDING YOUR IDENTITY WHY AM I HERE?

As we begin to draw the curtain on the attributes of your identity, we conclude this part by looking into a couple of fundamental attributes that God bestowed man with at creation.

- He created me to be like Him:
  "Let Us make man in Our image, according to Our likeness... So God made man in His image..." (Genesis 1:26-27).
- He gave me Purpose:
  "let them have dominion over... all the earth" (Genesis 1:26).
- He gave me Work:
  Then the Lord God took the man and put him in the Garden of Eden to tend and keep it. (Genesis 2:15).

Notice the order of the attributes God gave man at creation; He gave him identity before He gave him purpose. He gave man purpose before He gave him work.

Your Purpose and Your Work Come from Your Identity

Why did God follow this order? Your purpose is locked up in identity. Locked up in your purpose is your work. What does this mean? When someone gives you an object you've never seen before, what comes to your mind firstly is not the purpose or usage of the object, it is the identity of the object. You will first ask, "What is this?" Not, "What does it do?" or "How does it work?" If you can identify the object as a cellphone, then you can understand its purpose and how it works. But if you can't identify the object, you won't understand its purpose, let alone use it. No matter how valuable the phone is, it will be useless to you if you cannot tell what it is.

To discover your purpose and work, it is important you first discover your identity.

- Your identity is who God created you to be.
- Your purpose is what He created you to do.
- Your work is becoming what God created you to become and doing what God created you to do.

Let's go back to our illustration again. This object is created to be a phone. Its purpose is for communication. Using it to call, chat and do other phone-like activities is the work of the phone.

There are a huge number of working-class people struggling with their current jobs. Regardless of how much they earn, they are still not happy with their jobs. The reason is a misalignment between their identity, purpose and work.

This illustration will explain the alignment between identity, purpose and work.

A fish can swim because it is a fish.
A bird can fly because it is a bird.
To **do** it, you must first **be** it.
The reason why you are struggling to do it is because you are not it.

Your Ability comes from Your Identity

God put abilities in identities.

He put the ability to swim in the fish.

He put the ability to fly in the bird.

He will certainly put in you the ability to do what He created you to be and to do.

When God gave you an identity, He matched it with your ability.

Locked up in your identity is your ability.

Your Strength comes from Your Identity

Your identity determines the area of your strength.

The lion is strong: true, but only in the jungle. In the sea, the lion is weak.

The shark is strong: true, but only in the sea. In the jungle, the shark is weak.

You are strong: true, but only in your identity. Outside your identity, you will be weak and vulnerable.

As a leader, the key to building a successful workforce is to identify individual strengths in your team members and match those strengths with their job descriptions. When you give a member of your team a task they have no strength for, it will create a mess and leave them frustrated.

When your work is not aligned with your identity, you will always be frustrated with your work. Consistent mental fatigue may indicate that your work is not aligned with your abilities and who God created you to be. Conversely, a sudden rush of excitement when you are asked to do something, even when you are physically tired, could likewise be a pointer that your identity and ability are both aligned to that activity.

If you want to enjoy your work in the same way that I have enjoyed writing this book, then you must discover your God-given identity. Once you are able to do that, then the right work will follow.

5

THE IMPORTANCE OF YOUR IDENTITY WHY DO I NEED TO KNOW THIS?

It Protects You from Abuse.

Myles Munroe said, "if the purpose of a thing is not understood, abuse is inevitable." But as we have learnt that identity precedes purpose, we can also say that if the identity of a thing is not understood, abuse is also inevitable.

The word "abuse" is a combination of two words; "ab" (which means "away from") and "use". So the word "abuse" is "to use wrongly or in an improper way". Therefore, if the identity and purpose of a thing is not understood, that thing will be used improperly.

I strongly believe that gender-based violence, especially against women, is based on the ignorance of the woman's true identity. Stereotyping against women is as old as mankind. It emanates from an age-old cultural, religious, racial and patriarchal misconception and misconceived definition of who the woman is.

Men - commonly the perpetrators of verbal, physical, and sexual abuse against women - are ignorant of a woman's true identity, especially from God's perspective. When you understand her true identity - that she is a reflection of God's image and likeness - you will adore her, not abuse her. If you see her as a person, not as property, you will love her, not loathe her. If you see her as a helper of destiny, not a usurper of power, you'll appreciate her, not tolerate her. If you see her as the most intelligent of our species, you will cherish her, not maltreat her.

To accept that the woman is created in the image of God, after His likeness, is to accept that she's equal to the male gender. God is not gender-biased; He created the woman in the same class as man. Genesis 1:27 says, **"male and female He created them."** To reject this truth is to reject God's Word. To deny this truth is to deny God's Word. To fight this truth is to fight God's Word. Scripture cannot be broken; "male and female He created them", and God does not create second-class!

Your body as a child of God is also worth protecting from abuse. Why? 1 Corinthians 3:16 states that your body is God's temple. Therefore, God living in you makes your body worth protecting from abuse. The apostle Paul asked a couple of questions concerning the identity of our bodies as children of God. He said, "now the body is not for sexual immorality but for the Lord, and the Lord for the body.... do you not know that your bodies are members of Christ? Shall I then take the members of Christ and make them members of a harlot? Certainly not! *"Do you not know that your body is the temple of the Holy Spirit who is in you, whom you have from God, and you are not your own?" 1 Corinthians 6:13, 15&19.*

Paul went on further to say in Romans 12:1, "I beseech you therefore, brethren, by the mercies of God, that you present your bodies a living sacrifice, holy, acceptable to God, which is your reasonable service." Paul was implying that if you cannot identify your body as God's temple, you cannot use it for God's purpose. If you don't know who you are and whose you are, you will give in to anything and to anyone. But if you know who you are and whose you are, you will protect what you have - your body!

It Helps Your Spiritual Development & Maturity.

One of the ways we measure mental development and maturation in children is in their ability to identify objects. When you place a pencil in the hands of a toddler, it goes straight into the mouth. Why? The baby cannot identify the object (as a pencil), or its purpose or usage. That's why it is clearly written on some medicines, "keep out of the reach of children" because, to a child, any object could be food. But let that same toddler grow to an age where he has been taught to identify objects and give him that same pencil, he will look for a book to draw or write on. The child has now acquired the ability to identify a pencil as an instrument for writing not snacking.

Paul said, *"when I was a child, I spoke as a child, I understood as a child, I thought as a child; but when I became a man, I put away childish things." 1 Corinthians 13:11.* God measures our spiritual maturity by our ability to discover our identity, purpose and work in Christ. He also measures our spiritual maturity by our ability to identify the wrong things of life and avoid them, and to identify the right things of life and live up to them.

The moment you understand your identity in God, you will stop answering to the negative opinions people have about you. Why? Because you are not who or what they say you are; you are who and what God says you are. You will also stop trying to be like someone else; rather, you will strive to be the best that God created you to be!

The discovery of your spiritual and godly identity helps your spiritual development and maturity. A child can answer to any name but an adult answers only to his or her own name. You are who and what God says you are; answer to that! That is maturity.

It Protects You from Deception.

Jesus said, "The thief does not come except to steal, and to kill, and to destroy" (John 10:10). The devil is an identity thief. He comes to steal, kill and destroy identities of people. What led to the fall of Adam and Eve when they ate of the forbidden fruit, was their ignorance of their God-given identity.

The whole of Genesis chapter three gives us a picture of how the devil deceived Eve into eating the forbidden fruit, using her ignorance of her God-given identity. Take a moment and read what the devil said to Eve.

> *"Then the serpent said to the woman, "You will not surely die. For God knows that in the day you eat of it your eyes will be opened, and you will be like God, knowing good and evil". So when the woman saw that the tree was good for food, that it was pleasant to the eyes, and a tree desirable to make one wise, she took of its fruit and ate. She also gave to her husband with her, and he ate"*
> *- Genesis 3:4-6.*

The devil said to Eve, "If you eat the fruit, you will be like God." So Eve ate the fruit because she thought it would make her be wise like God. When I meet Eve, I have just two questions burning in my heart to ask her. These questions are;

- "Sister Eve, you were created in God's image and likeness. You were created a god-being. How could eating a fruit make you become who you already are?"

- "Sister Eve, you were created a spirit-being and one of the attributes of your spirit is wisdom. You were created wise. How could eating a fruit make you become what you already are?"

The devil is still using this same strategy to exploit a lot of women and men today. He uses their ignorance of their identity to make them needy of affirmation. So many women are entangled in abusive relationships because her claim is; "Oh, but he makes me feel like a woman." The question is, "What were you before?" So many men are trying to please unpleasable women, running themselves into debts because they claim, "It will make me seem more like a man to her." The question is, "What were you before?" Genesis 1:27 says, **"...male and female He created them."** How can something that someone does to you make you feel like what you already are? Yes, there are things we can do in our relationships to make each other happy and feel loved. But there is nothing you can do to make a man or woman feel more like a man or woman; God already made them that.

Girls who grew up lacking love, intimacy, affection, affirmation and security from their parents, especially from their fathers, will have a tendency to seek affirmation from other men. This will also make them vulnerable to falling into unhealthy and abusive relationships. They mistake lust for love; a kind gesture for intimacy; and a bar of chocolate for affection. The need for affirmation is the basis of control. The moment you look to people for affirmation, you give them the power to control you. You also surrender what you feel about yourself (good or bad) to human opinion.

The Good News is, Colossians 2:10 says *"You are complete in Him, who is the head of all principality and power."* God made you complete. There is nothing anyone can add to make you more or less of what God made you. Do not allow the devil to deceive you into trying to do anything to become more of who God created you to be. The devil is and has always been a liar. Let God's Word be the basis of your affirmation. Take your identity from His Word, not from human opinion. Stop trying to please people or to live your life based on their opinion. Rather, strive to be all that God wants you to be.

Psalms 139:14 says that you are wonderfully and fearfully made. The nicest compliment that anyone can pay you is just an affirmation of what you already know about yourself. And no one can call you a mistake because God does not create mistakes, He only creates miracles. You are that miracle!

It has always been the devil's bid to ruin the human race for generations; the ignorance of our God-given identity has always been his greatest weapon of deception and exploitation. Therefore, discovering your God-given identity in Christ frees you from both human and satanic deception.

It Protects You from Satanic Oppression.

In Acts 19:11-16, the devil victimized seven brothers because of their inability to answer a question about their identity. Acts 19:15-16; *"And the evil spirit answered and said, "Jesus I know, and Paul I know; but who are you?"* Then the man in whom the evil spirit was leaped on them, overpowered them, and prevailed against them, so that they fled out of that house naked and wounded."

Note the question, "...who are you?" In other words, identify yourself? But since they could not answer the question of their identity, the story ended with these men being badly beaten, wounded and humiliated by the demon.

Please understand that the devil oppressed them not because they did not know Jesus or Paul but because they did not know who they were. The devil can use what you don't know about yourself to oppress you. 2 Corinthians 2:11 says, *"...lest Satan should take advantage of us; for we are not ignorant of his devices."* Ignorance of your identity is dangerous; it gives the devil grounds to oppress you. In Hosea 4:6, God said, *"My people are destroyed for lack of knowledge."* Ignorance is a lack of knowledge.

The devil can use what you don't know about yourself to destroy you. Satanic oppression thrives on the platform of human ignorance. The devil is as strong as your level of ignorance and the devil is as weak as your level of knowledge. The strength of the oppressor is the maintenance of ignorance.

Why would God say that even His own people are destroyed for lack of knowledge? Here is the answer. 2 Corinthians 5:21 calls you, **"... the righteousness of God in Christ Jesus."** But Proverbs 11:9 says, *"through knowledge the righteous will be delivered."* So, a righteous man who is blood-bought, blood-washed and Spirit-filled can still be bound if he remains ignorant of his identity in Christ.

The first attack by the devil on the first man God created was an attack on his identity. The first attack by the devil on God's first begotten Son, Jesus, was on His identity *(Matthew 4:3-6 "if you are the son of God, turn this stones into bread").*

If the devil attacked Adam and Eve's identity, attacked Jesus's identity, he will surely attack your identity. The knowledge of your identity (who you are in God), is what will deliver you from such attack.

It is one thing to know who Christ is; it is another thing to know who you are in Christ. It is one thing to be saved; it is another thing to know what it means to be saved. Giving your life to Christ brings salvation but it is your knowledge of who you are in Christ that brings complete freedom and deliverance. *"And you shall know the truth, and the truth shall make you free." John 8:32.*

Now that you are aware that the ignorance of your identity could be a tool in the hands of the devil to oppress you, then you should never go to bed with a head void of knowledge of who you are in Christ. Choose to start every day with a head full of knowledge of who you are in Christ. A head without knowledge will be a burden on the neck!

It sets the next generation free.
In Acts 19: 16, seven brothers were victimized and oppressed by the devil because they were ignorant of their identity. I have always imagined that if the first-born knew his identity, he would have been able to free himself and his younger brothers from such humiliating experience. When I play this scene in my imagination, I picture the impact of this oppression to be more severe on the last-born. Why do I say this? You can't compare the strength of a child to an adult. Therefore, the beating that renders an adult unconscious could kill a child.

The knowledge of your identity is of utmost importance. Why? The consequences of your ignorance could have a greater impact on your children. The giants you refuse to conquer today might become greater ones for your children to conquer. The crises you refuse to deal with today might become greater ones for your children to deal with. It was the ignorance of the first parent on earth (Adam and Eve) that put the whole human race in trouble.

6

NATURE
INFLUENCES ABILITY
I CAN BECAUSE I AM

The "I am" precedes the "I can". The "I am" also determines the "I can". It means nature determines ability. You have to BE it first, before you can DO it. A fish can swim because it is a fish. A bird can fly because it is a bird. When you discover God's nature in you, then you will know what you can do.

Paul said, *"I can do all things through Christ who strengthens me." Philippians 4:13.* Paul was speaking from an understanding of the attributes of God's nature vested in him. God's spiritual nature in you gives you the ability to do what He has created you to do in life

Conclusion

The answer to all identity crises and low self-esteem lies in discovering your identity in God. Doing this will help you realize where to focus your strength. It helps you to do what God has enabled you to do, to be all that God wants you to be and to deliver you from the people-pleasing trap. It will also help you to say "YES" to the things that will help nurture God's nature in you and say "NO" to the things that will destroy God's nature in you. The reason why the human race went into captivity was because Adam and Eve could not say "NO" to what the devil offered to destroy their godly nature.

Because you are created in God's image and likeness, you are a blessing, not a curse. You are a solution, not a problem. You are an asset, not a liability. You are an addition, not a subtraction. You are a contribution, not a depletion. You are the light of the world and the salt of the earth.

Now that you have discovered your identity and who you are in Christ, it is time for you to break barriers, conquer limitations, exceed expectations and break new records for Jesus. Go - BE & DO all that God has created you to BE & DO.

With this understanding of your identity, the sky is no longer the limit to what you can become in life; it is just the starting point. SPREAD YOUR WINGS AND FLY!

God bless you!

Michael Ayeni.

VISIONARY LEADERSHIP

AUTHOR: MICHAEL AYENI

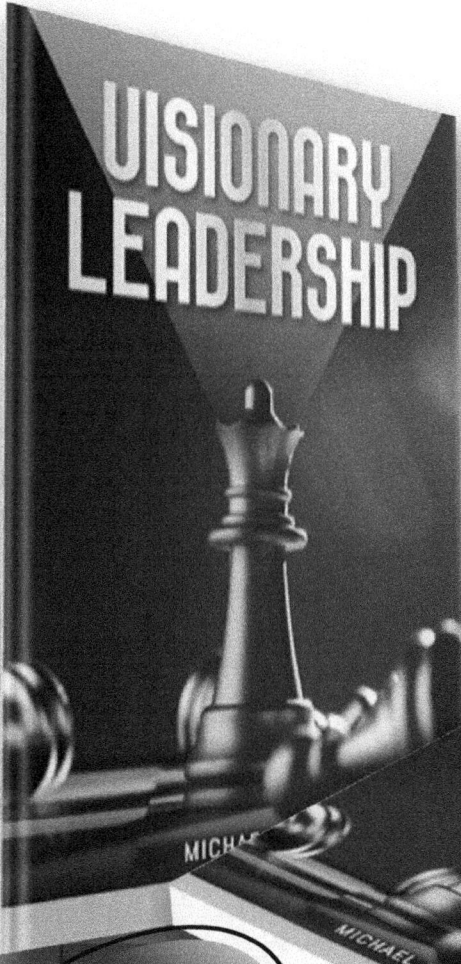

"Success in leadership does not happen by chance or coincidence, it is a product of Visionary Leadership.

Lack of vision is a recipe for failure.

This book provides the roadmap to succeeding in any position of leadership."

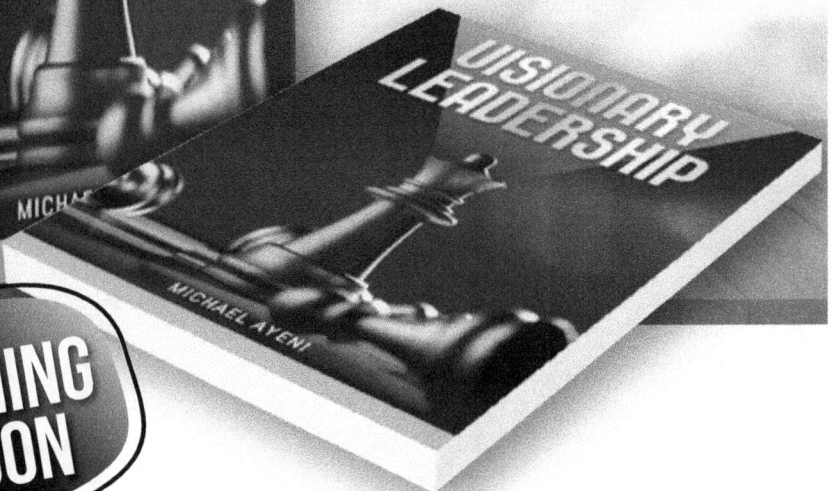

COMING SOON

www.ingramcontent.com/pod-product-compliance
Lightning Source LLC
Chambersburg PA
CBHW050949030426
42339CB00007B/355